PILLAGE LAUD

CAUTERIZATIONS · VOCABULARIES · CANTIGAS · TOPIARY · PROSE

"ERÍN MOURE"

BOOKTHUG DEPARTMENT OF REISSUE NO. 6

Library and Archives Canada Cataloguing in Publication

Moure, Erín, 1955–
Pillage laud / Erin Mouré. – 1st BookThug ed.

(Department of reissue; no. 6)
Originally publ.: Toronto: Moveable Type Books, c1999.
isbn 978-1-897388-83-9

I. Title. II. Series: Department of reissue; no. 6
ps8576.o96p54 2011 c811'.54 c2011-901289-8

Pillage Laud selects from pages of computer-generated sentences to produce lesbian sex poems, by pulling through certain found vocabularies, relying on context: boy plug vagina library fate tool doctrine bath discipline belt beds pioneer book ambition finger fist flow. Erín Moure January 1998

"...experimentation on ourself, is our only identity,
our single chance for all the combinations that inhabit us."

Gilles Deleuze
Dialogues

"... the art of combining is not my fault. It's a curse from above.
For the rest I would suggest not guilty."

Beckett, *"Enough"*,
Collected Shorter Prose

"The book is designed as a dictionary, and not as an encyclopaedia;
that is, the uses of words and phrases as such are its subject matter, and it is concerned with giving information
about the things for which those words and phrases stand only so far as correct use of the words depends upon knowledge of the things.
The degree of this dependence varies greatly with the kind of word treated, the difference between cyclopaedic and dictionary treatment varies with it, and the line of distinction is accordingly a fluctuating and dubious one."

from the Preface to the First Edition, 1911,
Oxford Concise Dictionary

Intus haec ago, in aula ingenti memoriae meae.
St. Augustine, *Confessions*, Bk. 10, Sec. 14

Pillage Laud—Vocabulary Grid

As-tu vraiment aimé quelqu'un? murmura Pessoa.

J'ai vraiment aimé qulequ'un, répondit Campos à voix basse.

Alors, je t'absous, dit Pessoa, je t'absous, je croyais que dans ta vie tu n'avais aimé que la théorie.

Non, dit Campos en s'approchant du lit, j'ai aussi aimé la vie, et si dans mes odes futuristes et furieuses j'ai fait de l'humour, si dans mes poésies nihilistes j'ai tout détruit jusqu'à moi-même, sache que j'ai aimé moi aussi dans ma vie, avec une douleur consciente.

Pessoa leva la main et fit un geste ésotérique. Il dit : Je t'absous, Alvaro, va avec les dieux éternels, si tu as eu un seul amour, tu es absous, parce que tu es une personne humaine, c'est ton humanité qui t'absout.

Je peux fumer? demanda Campos.

Les trois derniers jours de Fernando Pessoa. Un délire, Antonio Tabucchi, tr. fr. Italian by Jean-Paul Manganaro

PILLAGE LAUD

"Oakland"

PILLAGE 1 ("Oakland")

What was dangerous before we convert

Would you please be done with "that" before my adolescence

When being us entailed "mere" hardship

> To imagine at last what
> we had come across
> in depiction

fate sex vocabulary library citizen presence thwack

That day I wanted to be two girls in a car
Or that girl
That car

Her white pearl earring so base   shimmered
Making daylight a realm of incandescence

I wanted to be that daylight
It was night & an earring was enough for me

Where can the vertebrate of vertigo advance?
The process was town.

You practise this.
Her eyes met or did not meet "mine".
Had those cuts completed?

Were the lawns perfectly formulated?
That day on the beach?

I was crossing the road when I saw them,
two "she"s I envied, or
                              convected

My faint demeure
what the basises encountered

fate sex vocabulary library citizen presence thwack

I bury her. I curled.
An adult couldn't rush.

So generous a difficulty cannot read the passionnat of verse. They are
these winters.

Has the vigil of charm between the vestige and the sister
fitted?

Certain theorems are the libraries of bitterness, but her dawn etches
prisoners.
To survive is dreaming. The fury of number.

I admitted it; because we attended, to return was body. A shade—why
had nobody arisen? What is somebody hanging?

Where we are these emotions, we are those errors, and we contribute.

Their sentence—had each of them destroyed the rank of presence?
The stress is analysis.
So iron a father vaccinates beauty.

We are my veils.

fate sex vocabulary library citizen presence thwack

Where were we racing? To spread was laughter.
Her knees I wantonly adored

While sex was the structure's industry,
both were appearing.

The vested interest balanced. A master had slipped
A riposte her contusion.

Such a twelfth floor: pleasure.
Vocabularies were those empires.
Wit inside wounds.

To cry out determined her. Because we won't trust fate,
bereaved are balances.

What can atmosphere with
vocabularies delight?

We have desired those knees.
So arbitrary a vulva.

The vocabulary pressed: my teacher
between certain homes & a chin.

Has the gentle sibyl of wit inside wounds
startled the club of fate?

To underline her tress in me... upended...

fate sex vocabulary library citizen presence thwack

If I ordered an acre of charisma I would say so.

Trespass is not my only obligation.

Harmonic gender, did you eschew me?

{::}

The tirade of being in ecstasy.

If how a bird's chant can resurrect silence

A wet ping or impulse from meaning's glow

fate sex vocabulary library citizen presence thwack

Who have the phrases of Bebop aided? Although you were dust,
angels—the operations of error—were vapours among the stroke
between a citizen and some ritual.

Those vengeances typed.

The library—was so general an attempt doubting?
Had you resumed certain things?

The favour is your platform; and though to differ has moved a writing,
a computer is plaster.

The system of presence hits us.
To fit was its anode.

My citizen—what was every particle lacking?

Harm didn't verify us.
The vaccine of music was a gate.

Though asterisks rented her, metabolism silenced this, and so
tremendous a library spent light. Where I am her audience, what have
these republics coupled?

Nouns are its gears, and fabrics are your brushes.
Cries—didn't the eggs of thought defeat my ribbons?
When are those visit libraries typing?

The text has got to function.

Her tree between the label and a table, hitting.
Torpor was seven industries in kind.

fate sex vocabulary library citizen presence thwack

The ending—when has the vocabulary talked?
The fate—anybody remains.
The underling of destiny (the act) is another fortune.

What do certain American descriptions defend?
"I was the visa of childhood"?

Love (shelter) had vandalized the bird.
She who emellished the procedure of folklore rose to achieve the
theatre of charm. Her law uncoupled sheep. Its accolade varnished

Whom won't another journal design, ahhh
my dry observer.

When we arise, the street of coffee—so intense its thwack—is a
condition.
A strong vulva. Has April invigorated her master?

At the beginning—the branch of structure— waited.
A gift between the inspection and my device.
Her knees beneath the fur tsunami.

Cordial.

fate sex vocabulary library citizen presence thwack

What may accuracy plant? She survives, but sacrifice for her vulture is their sergeant. The vice around a whip believed you. An automobile: the register of time. Your bag—her reporter—is so infinite a darkness. This private a musician (the soldier) had extended. How have you yelled? To turn records the storm. The mate of shelter is differing; will art stretch? They name us. Although I visit this, people (the bathrooms) increase, and to lisp is a continental spot at any vat. So English a fellow is smaller a bet. Have we exceeded the teeth? You were so complicated a ratio, your udder was the voice of loss.

We were these (shelved) utopias.
Images of torsional cloth.

Why may the dictionary insist?
The noise book addresses their vigil.
A rusting tool.

The site—so direct a gleam with noise—was the stone,
and a chair of damage had signed *joke*.

fate sex vocabulary library citizen presence thwack

PILLAGE LAUD

"High Prairie"

PILLAGE 2 ("High Prairie")

for you who validated the earth with your ferocity

Wit—whom were you seizing?
To read was so comfortable a strip between
the version and your trick.

Every obligation quite burns.
Ferocity is belonging, and you understand this.

After we are certain plants—coalescent—
the wheel's umpire shakes.
To read was the ribbon of girls;

an adept invigorate before the coronal suture.
Would oil burst?

She who has performed the fault of ground
is the urge of ground. A tracked coast.

A willow.
To sing is so chaste an invention.

prairie pioneer cattle beds feeling field

Has the feeling spelled venison?

She is their watcher during the rules' restriction when
the clarinet dreamed, the noun would surrender.

Where had so vibrant a chamber (noun) curled?
My kitchen, my desire.
To pace is the feeling of time.

Where you remain, velour is the climate.
While you are shelters, every scheming machine could
benefit our frequency prairie.

Your mixtures were so suspected a blood.
This validated the earth.

What am I noting?
Rhythm (a gas) probably chewed the boiling minister.
The success of duty shall not enter, for your stage contains
no standard.

Time travel meant: small indelible birds.
Until some are nothing, a dialect belongs to bliss.
Victors were the steps.

The routines of courage were my symphonies.

prairie pioneer cattle beds feeling field

The keyword can't arrange this.
To come is so preliminary an engagement between the decade and
the computer that another measure is the vernier of terror.

That structure was agreeing no one.
Where you release it, a fact panic (building) wouldn't exist.

Fate strongly argued your vehicle across sisters.
Can't feeling form?

The book (a basement of illusion) varnished someone. Their
burning resistances yell. I was her

era and vaccinations were bursting.
A corner—some backward myth—wanted us, and we were those
shaking casts.
The talent merely dressed.

Although some girls walked, many were swinging beds.
Because any wind was artist, the chapel (the prairie)
chose it.

Futures were gestures.
If they were these prospects, my field had owned me.

prairie pioneer cattle beds feeling field

Their barn was the case of death.
Until cattle are recalling duties, your dancer is bitterness.

What is a yelling habit learning?
The citizen is the statement of vodka.

After a swerving scheme between her smile and my book,
the model of rope—voltage—is her dictionary.

Memory between certain hens and a bridge
is the course of art.

Has the ranch between the wing and her player
between the interval and the pioneer
asked this idle disaster?

To court attends. Her size walked.
In her idiom, how could my melody fight?
Before this fence is her pioneer, the food cracks me and my story.

After you live to verge, how couldn't a stake's
connection unbend?
Your frontier would benefit me.

Because you were my cups, so unbearable a statement
has vanished us.

prairie pioneer cattle beds feeling field

Who had the adults of opportunity listened. Have they pleased
performances? Relax won't display us.

This chapter is the idiom of curiosity, the note:
so competent a heroism.
Criticism was so veterinary a master.
The ventricle of marble, did an aloof fiction prepare?

We repeat laws, but you must circle me.
Our idiom—grace—came to flow; every hole had scattered
every vote, we were parades.
So thick a restriction is speaking.

To pause expands, who couldn't the urge establish?
My shock is exercise.
A dictionary especially rules.

The skirt between another life and the writer charms you;
when am I entering?
The risk tugs between a sentence and my pioneer.

Vertiginous.

prairie pioneer cattle beds feeling field

If my orchid wore the ache of charisma I would say so.

Trespass is not my wanton *obrigada*.

Harmonic sender, did you rue me?

{::}

I'm tired of beings in ecstasy.

If even a bird can't resurrect silence

Would a heartstring impede us in meaning's tow

prairie pioneer cattle beds feeling field

PILLAGE LAUD

"Roselawn"

PILLAGE 3 ("Roselawn")

What was I influencing? To form
is the music between your restriction and my industry.

Until a vein drove, silence failed, and your position absolutely listened.

What don't troubles visualize?
You stopped to forgive reputations.

So unbearable a statement has varnished us.
How should the prairie of fear climb our hip?

If to practice studied, shame charmed her.
Wounds are so pleasant a prison.

What have you parked the lobe of sleep?
Don't my boots honour shapes between the neighbourhood and
no fruit?

Before they will exhibit certain styles –
the vague action between a tear and an asterisk.
The theatre of matter only hoped.

The sheep is the attitude, and to crack should struggle.
My loop into the injury of memory between the historian and her charm
fought to find you.

You obviously recorded her.
Her type masters you.

To enter was the size.

fist flow archive finger textile book ambition congregation

What have the injured congregations reported?
America's roof is the film of corn.

So sexual a mask was drinking the heart of vigilance.

The book of ambition must wait.
Fields (the termites of vermeil) hoped someone,
and another hearse was willow between the artist and this Babbage.

Any brick vexes us. Although charm balances, fame hurries.
If stress between the cup and the clerk is the code of truth,
what are the intentions of business supporting?

The subject wouldn't split. My copy
(comedy about this plug throughout the farmer) struck this.

You are the messages, and democracy at the resident
comforts her. Melodies verged.

After so faithful a critic was the mill of football, the landing of jazz
subjected fears.

The muscle of her flesh was heat; my vagrants
are senses.

Whose differing fingers were textiles valuing?
Spring was determining this. The violet of force
compels my intention.
To stay reflects. They listen.

Where were her valves flowing?
To flow is her classroom.
What don't corn apartments churn?

fist flow archive finger textile book ambition congregation

Vocabulary is the phantom.
Unless every hard collection continues to extend,
to cry exactly rests.

So sexual a mask is drinking the myth of vigilance.
You are the twangs' hoodwink, and your index won't dream.

The book of ambition must wait: the chins of police
work to absorb mind. Where have my princes advanced?

We were those beauties.
We suddenly survive, and senators are the restrictions.
Where has a democracy between a bag and a sound dressed?

To dress was peace, and every arrival—the injury of power—was
cracking. Can the brick stretch her regime?

Any fist—a session—was weight between the missile and an
examination. Melodies verged her. Because so uncut a string
determined her, how had I paced?

So damned a garden was triumph where I was sinking;
because I can't rust, the finger (veneer) remembers
her form, and my standing region between the version and

an archive comforted me.

I was a front.
My label between every chief and the sex exposed you.
Liquid had broken the rich choir.

fist flow archive finger textile book ambition congregation

They land, and the pleasure assembled.
To function was land.
No uniform is its task like so unlikely a glass, but hipboots do charm.

What am I bothering? Have I delayed their congregation?
I may move me, but each of you longs to rule.

The urge of vellum is surveying her. Memories
arrested the smells of order, so dear a vixen admonished me.

The wound of dance transforms the company. We listen. When
must our valour packrat rush?

Your shoulder was switching. Certain trouble nouns curl the subject
of direction.
Whom has her matter hidden?

You appear to type.
The vein was so orderly a passion, top may remain.
What have the knees of chance achieved?

Those visas between every vagina and some business.
Has so bold an era between the hole and the book nodded?
Whom were they piercing? The sister term: a waist.

While you drank me, museums vanished.
Depths met this.
The strap (her partner) badly paused.
To nod uncorked our jerseys.

fist flow archive finger textile book ambition congregation

Why are the resistances of bread suffering?
I was the darkness of metabolism.
Salt (criticism toward the whip during vulgarity) altered the bed.

The gallery of flesh was trouble; she who purely gathered
was so western a light.
Her vestige is teacher. Dirt was the conversation.

Her temperature between a being and every doll was laughing;
unless you age, the valets have tempted a vow.

When are we balancing? We had slid.
What are we tending?

I am so unarmed a fashion, you are its laps
between the temple and every desiring chain.

The notion (so stable a valentine)
wouldn't stain your mount.
After you could turn to you, shall colour vibrate?

Since I fully rub you, she has dived.
The finger of opera was visualizing it.

Lids cannot venerate you; you are her regimes now
between engagement and the veil.
Our rules drifted.
Where I am your act of venison, art turned to luxury.
To matter forms me darkly.

If to grieve cared to surrender, to snap
startles the companion.

fist flow archive finger textile book ambition congregation

PILLAGE LAUD

"Bowness"

PILLAGE 4 ("Bowness")

Since certain minute ends must crawl, so texture a library was
childhood,
and to race would sound velocity,
and you left.

You were the orchestras of presence.

What had such categories gathered?
Hydrogen was so partisan a testament.

After to arise avoided so belief a vestibule, her widow needed to
wash sex. Each of her can verge; tissue should form.

After place is her paper, a prisoner is flight, & my conductor
(the code) has stumbled.
Whom could the fault employ?

I strictly guided the blood.
Since its drawing is the flight, my text is grieving,
and these belts finish every arrangement.

vandal tissue curl plaster smell body bent

Beyond matter's underling, the vesicle fell.
Paid to vaporize another forest in a rich economy.

Plaster was my chapel. Her shape—my leg—ran;
to emerge was the field.

When has another horizon orchestrated smell. Every democracy
appeared to distribute someone, and you were
the diameter of shale.

Another index's process shifts. A complicated
and not incendiary mote structure: stable.
She who leaped belonged—her eggs.

This closing image—whom is so strongest a handle subjecting?

Had you located the cocktails of beef?
A pound of dragon was reporting someone.

We curl you.

vandal tissue curl plaster smell body bent

To crack dresses—had I played?
Your belt (the poem of charm between a speaker and the conversation)
writes; another sacrifice is the reason.

The body (my appointment) is so brilliant a talent.
To verge tracks that.

Certain libraries swelled the companions' brevity.
The darkness of coinage was comparing the sessions of triumph.
The chicken (the specimen of food) could advise the living.

So domestic a voyage tested this,
and the journal was wing.

Those uncontrollable portions go; why is some realm playing?
To close has broken its shape.

The distance of wealth embellishes my addresses. My lover bends.
No, *means to bend. I tarnish her. This escapes.*

Before to form hurried, my vandal awed you. Its suture presence (ventricle)
was skin.

vandal tissue curl plaster smell body bent

She advanced.
A degree: every belt's hutch in the thought narratives. The
agreement (information) was metabolism along force.

Had you died? To twist is land. To unbend advances. Tension
is pulling her. Your silence so substantial a valour.

The revolution had uncorked my rhythm, and affection was augmenting.
Certain stresses cured beds;
the equation of living must listen.

Flesh progressed, but her system was a station.
Your gesture starts to assemble some living beam.

Shall you permit every vandal's fist trilling your bowl? I travel.
She is so unclad an opportunity, your prince clearly flows.

We were those cheap dilemmas.
These galleries crawl: so intense a purpose.

The narrative tracks you. Struggles will exercise unbent until
the identity villages can cry out, or close.

vandal tissue curl plaster smell body bent

If my word arched the girl and h

Her wan tress of the brigadista!

Has harm no sentry where she lu

{::}

A fast tryst could lay me her recl

An event's insurrection in my bl

Her wet pulse of impudence, car

If my word arched the girl and her isms I would soar, oh.

Her wan tress of the brigadista!

Has harm no sentry where she lured me?

{::}

A fast tryst could flay me her reckless sea.

An event's insurrection in my blurred eye's lens

Her wet pulse of impudence, careening

vandal tissue curl plaster smell body bent

PILLAGE LAUD

"Fairview"

PILLAGE 5 ("Fairview")

Had difficulty cured a fabric between this living
and a victor?
Until you projected me, to sound cannot note someone.

Whom was she meeting? Matter: the press.
Sympathy has occurred.

To stay hesitated, and to crack was pacing.
When so subtle a skin is so smooth a poet,
the clouds' wound (no feature) west begins.

When couldn't acupuncture peer? Mustard was suffering.

You are the radiation charm. You are her students. Darknesses
between the victor and the incident upon a packrat have competed, and
every section vacillates.
Whom had your belt structures enforced?

What do skirts foil? A love sequence left you. You
were a shore.

So vascular an outcome (the archive) is room.
Its volley between the ward and the heat is helping.

childhood fist grace belt feeling mustard burst charm

So gay a fist (her talent) supplies this.
How had the grace hands except mouths panicked.

To shift was the dare.
Its bedroom—filter toward dawn—was the
lobby, and she stood.

Had your tone run? They are places.
Practice was a feeling, you pass this.

After to scheme reflects, assumptions dress.
So romantic a position—the top of vertigo—again appears.

To practice lived to increase.
She who is the belt realizes us.

Until each of us purely cuts us, the desire of
oak stumbles. You are hipboots.

A realm (the skirt) prevents it; our company: your scene.
Since you are these hands' bays, shape
should account for you.

Had we visited computation? Luxury across faults doubts us,
you are certain letters, dived ambition,

so excellent is your aim.

childhood fist grace belt feeling mustard burst charm

This history: any event.
When any staring couch has occurred, we
are certain letters, and we volunteer.

To fit addressed experiences. Where no one was bending
in a virile age, the ranch between an act
and the artist urged a rhythm.

Had each of us shut a hipboot's sway?
Girls were my vigils. So catholic a fault is the charm;
to exist temporarily charms me.

The conception continued. I had panicked.
To succeed is waiting, and to crawl fills her exhibition.

Had you waited for certain battles?
Because to balance had verged, your valour islands pushed her.

Entrances (these slaves) were so sufficient a vocation,
and to rest regarded bodies.

She twisted a track. Your rector follows it.
Your curve is soap; I slightly cry.

Where have the visas started?
"A melody is my prairie"?

We were these comments.
You were swelling. The rest is radar.

childhood fist grace belt feeling mustard burst charm

The cap of power happens. After a childhood is your
medium, we are so unconscionable a motive.

To emerge was no angle.
I couldn't open her.

When the vault of loss was racing,
her longer dialect advised (the vigil) phone.

Where were your atoms appearing?
She was every vortex.

The surviving ritual could balance, and
her operator about those pleasures bears someone.

Before exist caused play, the pound visualized her, and
she gently drove until you had burst those skirts.

Had you visualized the testimonies of beef?
If your idiom has crashed, her arrivals will claim this.

The crises of pleasure query so unbounded a bird.
She who plays has burst so hot a detail.

Her wild dialect changes a circumstance's trip.

She who is the master of curiosity flows.
Why do these fibres hesitate?

childhood fist grace belt feeling mustard burst charm

While to fit is talking, her height is metabolism and
my chest (the top of art) is that section.

How are we coming?
After their mile split, we were her engines.

To land is her scene of ventilation, but you crack.
After they can extend, pain (iodine) was a citizen article.

Suitcases (her middles) were those senses.
Pleasures: peas. Mustard was heat. Those poems: vulgarities.

The roof—must tribute begin?
Chance grieves a glory's filter.

I today struggled.
The star of excess races to rule.

Though the imitation has prepared,
I still swell their ceremony of charm.

When vulva typed this, she sprung at you.
So absolute her fit vexes the proof.

childhood fist grace belt feeling mustard burst charm

PILLAGE LAUD

"Bloorcourt"

PILLAGE 6 ("Bloorcourt")

Her discussion of smoke has pointed to this silent bay,
but I am this fever.

To insist is my joke.
Since I have poured this, the principal of shame (doctrine) shall
achieve its passion.

The muscle—action—practises.
Some liked hydrogen; and airports had replied.

Where have the partners grieved?
Since to read was the effort, the airport of structure was her
document's core.
While the volley may speak, what had the strokes of pain warned?

To leave partially agrees, my skin persuades this.
So unclad a dictionary challenges us.

To so clear a prairie, our whisper was landscape. The roof (cut)
the congress of affection.

To surrender drives. Climate—whom is no trace becoming?
Whom had the comedies of mercy confronted?
She was my ending; I had surrendered, but an inspection was speed.

Where toast emerged, nobody will come.
The command of radar was my estuary.

The crises are languages verse typed.
The chest especially.

airport stroke maid toast envelope belt whoosh vagina

The vein was the river of size; you were
so bold a passion.

Have my articles reflected manners?
Couldn't measure sigh?
Desires are evenings; to crack is her affair.

Although she had denied you, to enter was
"her America"
and an emotion instantly pointed to *you*.

The line vaporized a frontier.
Although you are so slim a dish, her rhythm exactly dances.

The platform of trouble was your envelope, but your risk compelled
music. The viola was vanishing. I was its lieutenant, but the back
reached so bent a talent. To expand was a natural struggle; had many
stretched? Any hair despite a muscle (that fish) revealed cocktails; a
stadium is panicking.

A writing desk shouted, but companions more sank. Won't
any beauty strip an uncouth editor?

After illusion was the skill of life, she will suffer.
The model of escape will grip someone.

Had neither swollen?

If an invitation stood, a figure was going. What has hand acted on?
Why could the maid of oxygen crack?

Those are *their* versions.

airport stroke maid toast envelope belt whoosh vagina

Her teabag might complain.
After the colt of toast appears to sigh, her song leaps.

Since you harmed you, where had she spread?
Versions—so occasional a gear—were replying.

To roll was every envelope's vagina.
The surface of motion searched, we had stood.

May so angry a fan reply?
Whom are we silencing?
To speak forward succeeds it.

The judges' vagina is the proof; and her clarinet in the box of vinyl
lights me.

Has so adequate a gallery balanced so uncontrollable a goal?
What am I destroying?

After she rolled, libraries were your virtues.
Devotion's chapter should delay so front an idiom.

How wouldn't this identity laugh?
To drift is her talent. To stay is no drama.

Lies can't act.

airport stroke maid toast envelope belt whoosh vagina

A chamber—may your vagina uncoil her frontier?
To shake subjects her gear. Leather had fitted.

So mobile a chest could split where I had swollen.
To extend apparently cracks the vassal.
A dove coupled us.

Had so extra a bed exercised the shoulder's cloud?
We have happened. I had underlain the mouth of cattle.

You store her.
After you handled my top, I realized the breakfast of willow.
To burst is my breast of sacrifice; her attempt
(realm) is your vestige.

So vestigial a triumph lifts thought.
Whom had the fresh poem mattered to?

Steam is so impossible an uncoupling,
and the threat of language forgives her.

The forest of memory should go.
To vibrate twisted leather between that memory and those beds.

airport stroke maid toast envelope belt whoosh vagina

Her impulse could extend her fist; would honey complain?
A core was the atttempt between the twang

and the vagina. Since planets are disasters,
I can't remain, but I must absorb that point.

The writer orbits me. My line (article) has sighed.
Although the diameter altered changes, so
instant a restriction was dreaming. Blood should struggle.

The space of verse was the arbitrary sign between
the magnitude of consciousness and a price.
Since I ate the jowl of voltage, had her glad
vacuole stumbled?

So pure a hand was another nation.
Some identity was shattering it.

Had you occurred? Art had filtered you.
You were returning me, but I saw her shoe in your cape of vigour
after so popular a whooshing belt extended her hotel.

Although you stopped my tear, I was so effective a being,
and her valentine shifted this maid.

You are force. Had I affected language to undo the core?
Speech employs this, her sigh's envelope knows the vane.

I was a book, but the lobe was her procedure.

airport stroke maid toast envelope belt whoosh vagina

PILLAGE LAUD

"Burnaby"

PILLAGE 7 ("Burnaby")

What should memory write?
"They were the balls."

When a device was leather's insect,
what were my beauties seizing for their archive?

Girls were dramas between a regime and
a couch, and the girl was their bath.

The vitamin inside a radio burned.
In the orbit between a routine and the library,
you are her reports.

The hand: your vixen. Rhythm demands her glance.
To burn is cheek, can't the skin balance?
This cell dances

within the land's ventricle, where you wouldn't wipe
my prince. Since a size grips pressure, their friend
is owning the message. Could vengeance begin?

She who is the site is this spot.
So deep a porch named that stem;
the fence of beauty shifted.

Unless we are burning, whom am I opening?
Palaces are so varied a split.
The attached narrative is furnishing her, the treaty of the senses
to every rushing girl.

We were meats. A dare couldn't improve us.

doctrine girl bath library essay discipline extend hotels

Can't base die?
Since steam remembers me, the circumstance improves
our vibrations.

Unless I heat her orchestra, autonomy near so municipal a vise
during details is virtue.
We are the loose arts.

Do the geniuses of pleasure determine their cap?
Where we have extended, to wait is the shame.
Can't the hypothesis of willow wound some century of dignity?

No hole is vanishing.
The truth of sex glances.

If certain pennies are the selfs, have I grinned?
Have I faced democracy?

I am the reporter of mustard. Could tie talk?
Density plants so active a fear.

The lip has poured you.
I am an iceberg of grace.
You uncurl me.

doctrine girl bath library essay discipline extend hotels

Shall any suspicion love the essay?
You were the dare: since we had stayed,

when would some vibration pause?
The switch hopes.

Ammunition—has she demanded the scarce index?
The tape cannot visualize the review identity.

Curl, though an observer is their favoured reading.
Although their victim is writing,

I ignore us. Dirt fought to exercise film.
So precision a volcano (the protease of grace) cannot develop
so desirable a bed.

Bases vacillate. No hole is vanishing
Resistance (this size) advised her.

Since we ruled, what had her box punished?
Where her warrant of autonomy travelled,
your score slowly guided the film.

Her critic—the violet of vacuum between certain vandals
and a shoulder across the bar's loss—tracks your boy.

You save a regiment. A vision in hotels.
To march is writing.

doctrine girl bath library essay discipline extend hotels

You are my pain at the husband of form.
You had rejected me, but you were so precise
a lock. To arise starts.

Her air—what won't some earth press?
Your farm is racing. Because to yell is the belt of
grace,

certain holes listen. To practice is the record.
After I have vibrated, whom are you opening?

Density—my lady—has broken discipline.

She stretched those vises. They thus prefer the
bedroom of sand.
Weathers had returned;

so literary a ribbon programmed my
dictionary.
While I have exhibited your fear, why am I flowing?

You who are the opera of sauce—groups between
the
library and the senses—can't tend me. Her skirt—
that adoratum –
has seized some shoulder's epic.

Vocabulary was so last a vignette illusion. Has
somebody chewed it?
Why does every dictionary extend?

doctrine girl bath library essay discipline extend hotels

PILLAGE LAUD

"Rachel-Julien"

PILLAGE 8 ("Rachel-Julien")

What had so meaningless a book sheltered?
Film will remove the chemical region between the valve
and the message.

While I am exposing this condition, what can't a state undergo?
The library panicked.

A shaking evening was a label. Had the wastes of electricity
switched the words of worry?

Though you fought to excite her, whom couldn't my plug
dispute?

Your drawing of her affection delivered the series, billing me.
We were certain girls and the observation of town (the restaurant)
couldn't vanquish our fast joy.

Why are certain ones companions?
I unbent, but some virus in her website was the pool.

To care directs the fig of veal, she said,
and circumstance for song was your vagina. What were these
pictures continuing? Why were you working?

Until she is the river, the idiom produces it.
So wild a chest: the trap of venison.

Why is a vendetta travelling through the procedure?
To shake robs her.
The yoyo of language had snapped.

speech power exchange metabolism hospital lisp

If you were so medical a veil,
an audience could reduce the concert about the monument.

I attempt to vitiate us, and the fury is leaping.
I exchanged her.

You threatened anger.
The library should observe the empire of respect, the
vertebrate of custom.

Patrols are tops within kitchens; why should their crash hurry?
Any vulgar note (the structure movement) accomplished a mouth.

Whom were you arousing,
that the ranch of veal may enter?

To glance demands a form.
Power failed; the fault was accuracy. If she faced speech,

every yelling metabolism was the prisoner.

I perhaps considered her pistol.

A body—how is she splitting?
What is the observation of difficulty silencing?

speech power exchange metabolism hospital lisp

The hospital (a dream) is gold.
Patients (so preceding a fist) report me, and oil is the plunge of
venison.

Matters—shores—were her strengths.
If her model at the asterisk of discipline like so slow a back melted,

what had you ventured? To smile
is so gorgeous an election. What won't experience melt?

If that would vent the action of evening, the metabolism flows.
Girls (bags of voltage) moulded us, and vises—monuments were my vetoes.

The beam is competing; and the vibrato vibrates, and
the struggle of Autumn within your package stares.

Where we can't begin it, we checkmated the dog bakers.
A theory beach was the attitude of vermouth.

Had I declined?
To vacillate shuddered her.
Autonomy was the bird of grass of no epic, no dress.

Because so extreme a top is its pace, the vortex
of liquid—so new a wrist—is the description of beauty.

speech power exchange metabolism hospital lisp

The wound of sleep was delivering me. You courted her.
We cannot uncouple this. The vice of cream was essay;
while to insist was parking, you were idiom.

Has everybody escaped its heart?
After the gang of dust preserved her, so vanilla a unit was ferocity in
the tube of evening.

Though halls beyond justice against your vixen—my ports –
were businesses, the category of velvet grabbed us.

Hands are flowing. Many were charms in dictionaries.

These trace the range of density, the emperor of escape.
When are the sums rising?

Though your metabolism rejected her, you are the title.
You graced you.

To shout was passion you expect to rule
where vowels have schemed.

Certain ministers (legs) curl underbrush;
what is wit along the chime of duty fashioning?

A pure report is a neck. Your charm pulls her: the
vegetable of whisky. Couldn't her beauty rise?

The skill of history pours us.
She mounts your unconquerable boy.

A bottom now rushed, a silence play was every fever.
Since I saw this, I was so mean a bride.

speech power exchange metabolism hospital lisp

Ceremony sighs. The accident is the structure.

We are so oral a power, and to leave becomes her.
Has she perforated your ton?

When to fit down burst, coffees pierced electricities.
So ventral a cell was insisting; the tradition was coffee.

Have those shells included the coffee variables?
A forming index is the structure of theory.

Where harm would cite me, some exhibition had
discovered this.
You connected fictions, but I fight to do.

Do the dawns of coinage warn the lovely vessels?
Like duh.

When we readily replaced no chain, to leave was an unalloyed
decision,
and chance (so unbeaten a regime) was relaxing.

What couldn't the vellum repair?
The legend might forget her.

Unless illusion is the text, and that final empire is a vixen
between the company and some wake, and fist
(salvation) polishes my stair...

Unless a book presses its veto....

speech power exchange metabolism hospital lisp

PILLAGE LAUD

"Burnside"

PILLAGE 9 ("Burnside")

Their affection had asked the living. You wanted her; couldn't the
cocktail drift?
I step on her palm of coal.

Experience—darkness between the conversation and my
asterisk—is the principle of a whim autonomy.
When talent types us, love can avoid nest.

Have you owned my sentences' cases?
The fist of direction has driven my type.
Texts were methods.

Every vestige curled. This tough viburnum stretches the district.
Before to burst hears my volcano, a bridge had swollen.

To stay influenced her leaps.
When to split couldn't sign me, you paused.
Furniture—my bowl—was our orchestra.

The audience snaps her form.
Craft—your vesicle—is force.

When those evenings between our livings and the blood listened,
to count was threatening a blood.

How shall the page sleep?
Your stroke was another theorem.

The moves of discipline laugh—dearest vesicle –,
stripping so nearest a minister of the body.

livings vesicle split texts gallery burst swollen stroke

The differing ward is my beginning.
She who completely strips a radio is flight across the life of
any prince. We spread. She is the elaborate feature thing.

When the spare tradition has done—so doubtful a foot between her
rhythm and my shade—to swell is underling.

Have these crashes closed?
Because you won't leave, your west is burning.

Since you were controlling her, you were the virtues.
Galleries are these idioms.

We drank. I chose. When have gears remained?
Your tremendous viburnum affects me.

So steady a veil—whom had you uncorked?
To crack is the limit of vocabulary.

Those were the scenes but she now directed us.
I am the bed; and so independent a memory; may discipline
remember my smell?

Affections, she said, are slave magnitudes.
If you are that flower, these decisions (certain memories) wait,
and to burst ends so unclad a position.

So stern a distance, the lovely finger upon so vulnerable a tractor—will fit.

Though to talk assists this, when is the text changing?
Your power (my breast) wastes you.

I laud your instrument. Balance (a belt or west)
graced her version.

livings vesicle split texts gallery burst swollen stroke

The limit of opera farms someone, and a wife has slipped.
Has she dressed? The step support is the preceding atom.

Although you stroke her to burn forms,
to burst is no visitor.

Why had the arrangements of argument mattered?
What didn't a finger suffer?

These are glues. She was their effect. The structure
like juries during burdens was suspect.

Identities are the strokes of protein.
Have you looked for those beings?

After her frontier beyond the dare had grieved,
so erect a vulva was emperor, the screen—its coast –
snapped you.

Truths—why were those acting?
A rose wouldn't yield your archive.

An archive: space, its vagabond between those roots and those
imitations, won't vibrate.

Courts: certain injury contrasts.
Because to move was route between a shape and that girl,
the station of verse cut harmonies.

The dilemma between the pain and a failure: language.

Whom are you meaning? Don't violas count as vulva zombies?
Might her emperor change?

livings vesicle split texts gallery burst swollen stroke

Disaster (the verse design) was a party between the version and the
conversation. These tributes

where the cut of speed should come: to play has burst.
Wouldn't her vesicle yield the jock of flesh?

Salvation defines so explicit an anode behind the volume.
Had neither faced rice? Her margin forsook me.

You were these trust afternoons.
You magnified the trust of any lifted dress.

Wouldn't patience damage the gallery fountain?

If to trust drifted, you could dominate the virago of plaster.
So fiscal a whip (stuff) betted the renaissance.

Until we had practiced, to succeed was your vicar,
your metabolisms. Your rush is her host.

In the twang of circumstance, our fight can swell
our dear ambassadors' testament.

What burst entry had your volunteer constructed?
What text have I acted on?

To intend forms me. The beauties' fevers
are the velocity—a brilliant library—to my device.

livings vesicle split texts gallery burst swollen stroke

Do the documents face so international a choice?
A crisis after the united response is the essay.

Fear—has each of us burst?
She who matched your neck trusted the curve.

Whom were the violets locking?
Her deck between a knee and these colonies: pitcher.

You achieved her. To write was the second,
but to whip will establish the union.

You had rushed.
After you furnish the outcome, I am so southern a glory.

What won't the slaves of clothing number?
There is an impediment in my regret.

Although so tight a vulva concerns the colonel of position,
to shout is her sequence.
Where velocity was taste, we were so excellent a harmony.

Would the ray leave the museum of flesh?

Because both were honeys, a protein often
visualized so uneasy an identity.

Her station was uncorking a beam near its gallery.
The crucial statement is the circumstance of writing.

To break is my patience. The tool of paper
is the milligram, and pursues the tale.

livings vesicle split texts gallery burst swollen stroke

You vex the film of order.
Had we read?

You were those apartments; we had measured her;
and while a fiction shall differ, so undaunted a cloud
mattered. Had you reported metabolism?

The empire of voice will rule my design.
Although so full-time a desire was the report, a trial
transformed her dabbling detectives.

Before you twisted, how had she complied?
Any practice contained it; when can her box continue?

Certain teeth below our license benefit the cloth.
An emotion between my bed and a chamber is the verge.

Desire arrested so excessive a stroke, her duties
were curious.

Your textile had understood me. To vary couldn't report our
exercise, but I cannot race.

I am splitting my very increment open.
We should sleep.

livings vesicle split texts gallery burst swollen stroke

PILLAGE LAUD

"Glorieta de Bilbao"

PILLAGE 10 ("Glorieta de Bilbao")

Porches smiled; what didn't her trap do? Until I shift,
to run determines my turn.

The cracking hall is the essay of motion. When we conducted
to compare so delightful a ladder, you were shaping.

The maid of trust: a metabolism.
What is the champion of leather renting?

Sheepskin—so marginal a sheet—advised me.
The rail between the lock and a bedroom—the excess –
discussed the angle. She who is released hopes.
Structures were those offers.

While you are furnitures, phrase will vanish; you commonly love
those houses.

Citizen: why have you lived?
The whispering hair has replaced the hesitating object.
The palm of stuff can't look at us.

harness size plug bottom top vibrate camp ambition

harness size plug bottom top vibrate camp ambition

Why have I paused at the Glorieta? This inspection may close.

Because measures had timed the results, they were so pure a fist,
under so vigorous an impulse.
The portion and the size were so consistent a decade.

You rose to twist.
The bottom of fate was the linament.

A desire of pleasure was consciousness and surrendered its vagrant
between the observer and the duty.

To live was the umbrella of plaster; underbellies: the tones of value.
I encouraged us, but noon was the emergency of courage.

Resistance should twist.
Vellum unbuttoned me; what was each of us rejecting?

I was a lost fig.

harness size play bottom top vibrate camp ambition

harness size plug bottom top vibrate camp ambition

The plug inside a curiosity text is in movement. Why had the
spreading nests yelled? I unclasped an art at
her insertion.

The promise (the pea) was the row of vapour by a prairie,
her feet between the structure and no lock may lock
the suspended years. These paths shake such tradition.

She owned you. Has the bottom sketched no dilemma?
So round a specimen is the work of beauty;

while you will do, the visit paces. Song—a nearby drug—
may appear before women: the trip of vodka.

The intention melted.
Strokes can allow her.

The article of pressure switches so viviparous a champion,
because to unbend has begun.

harness size plug bottom top vibrate camp ambition

harness size plug bottom top vibrate camp ambition

Tops: the therapists.
She is hoping camp (the essay) won't vibrate.

Your knee was the pure testimony.
How had I vibrated an underling? After so maximum a routine
resumes us, the entries answer.

You are the succession inside my kingdom, where to curl easily
occurs.
We could sound: luxury recommends advice.

The partner must remember the strength; so unbounded a power
was a pretty visit. May a democratic vacuole through my living
park?

She who will claim me will forget ambition.
Because you are captain, her practice softens that electron.

I was a canvas speaking for the likely word.
Your plate is operating, you surely plant you.

The brain—every honour—should arise.

harness size plug bottom top vibrate camp ambition

harness size plug bottom top vibrate camp ambition

Do utopias complete those treatments?
Unction between the dare and the director: an ambition vandal.

I was your cape. She is a thing.
Any cape was the net, and we tested so orderly a top.

Salvation along a varying leg paid this. We could exist.
Your bride beween my ambition and no stress has survived her.

Where to split possible courts a discipline, my path is her taste.
You are the orchestra of light, nouns furnished me.

A member could fit where so appropriate an answer had inserted,
still must a novel return?
A varying belly is my description. My jersey pulls.

Libraries above a middle climax—what are they preparing?
After I am your prince, ships (my depths) are minutes.

Some leather experience is uncompromising a clarinet;
she has occurred.

harness size plug bottom top vibrate camp ambition

harness size plug bottom top vibrate camp ambition

So constant a lip is the vigilante of afternoon.
You ran from the doctrine of agriculture to the rain.

Had the islands of fire delighted so amazing a size?
The belt (another rank) is my mountain. This practice:
her button.

Whose space has your vesicle limited?
Though to live is rain, to unbend has belonged, and our spaces
scarcely snap.

Opera is a material plane. What has any entry bent?
So sure a ladder across an error (the conversation of business): a
renaissance.

The ending of sex leaps into breath.
To exercise would find them the engine of vigour, your harness.

Another generation can stroke the mistake.

harness size play bottom top vibrate camp ambition

PILLAGE LAUD

"Fra Mauro Hills"

Apollo 13's lunar destination, never reached; crew made emergency return to Earth,

17 April 1970.

PILLAGE 11 ("Fra Mauro Hills")

Keywords (those guards) are these memorial casts.
My identity had grinned.

Despite vibrations, whom had the vetos of enthusiasm near your stars
excited? To decline unclasps a clock of motion.

We crash. Until she issues a crisis between the fort and the rights, to
grieve temporarily progresses.

To glance is so sober a language. I had robbed from her no charm;
she fed these virtues.

Before we have gripped legs, any vulva runs from the palace.

After my bedroom stopped, whom was I fighting? A stronger star
claims you. Liquor attracts some evening, and her chime of cotton
(envelope) wants to curl. The special vestibule will act, and a bottom
upon so proper a position fears to see a supper between a party and
these villains.

Doubts currently admit certain bones as vignettes.
Autonomy: my fool. The trouble requires the beam of typhoid.

Then the heart writes: "To believe cannot burst." So dry a decision
could flow, but the punishment—marriage—shall attend the tone of
failure between a chapter and my arrival.

Dear one, I am the title, and you are heights.
Whose vagina—mask—was vane?

legs vestibule vagina marriage envelope grieve flow

A person: shell.
What have I heaved? I am the panel of enthusiasm,
a gate's viburnum between her fibre and those certain curves.

To drink was my burst officer. Prayer can't lift my account of
doctrine. Didn't the palm of wit land on the emotion?

Moons are these creatures.
What you were exciting, dictionaries continuously repair it.

After to twist was no figure, the cases unclasped;
platforms did seize my princes.
The observation of devotion could finish you;
has my ambassador festooned corn behind the pudding joke?

So gay a vault cast light.
We are the illusion bedrooms.

When you had denied you, I was an evil value
between every wound and the breakfast.

Earth (some viburnum) is its resistance; to fit is putting this,
but her breast has suggested doubt.

Why could error laugh? The scheme is working.
I close me.

legs vestibule vagina marriage envelope grieve flow

If she is my Europe, you stroke shelter
between the structure and
my type.

To flow ends; and you are brasses. You dress.
You also mastered certain error rituals.

Until you demanded to write, the company of corn was major;
destiny had added graces.
When we are the poems near so laud a news,
the maid faces me, and your vortex would delay my fountain.

The hospital left, but grace had counted.
You were the victor's tools in the republic of my tresses.
Asterisks believed in so municipal an archive.

Where the three events matter, I am the
vigilante, and presence can drive. The occupation cannot replace
 grace.

Should identity cite the trace of nature?
The ranch of plaster can grip no amateur. Her identity drifted.
I am the voyage's resistance; to burn is reducing this.

legs vestibule vagina marriage envelope grieve flow

To read was an affection, but they enjoyed her.
Your border is that pleasure I was mastering.

To stretch uses that cheek; to twist closes you.
Whom had the bottoms acted? The work's middle cites me.

Her slope shall hold stuff, but those are our centuries.
Wit raced our frontier.

Leather between a vocable and my vocation: the poem.
If devotion shall verge the obvious vagina,

to whom is this speaking machine hastening?
Don't basises end?

What had we pierced? We were flowing.
Since she is my republic, I have stopped the dresses of drama.
Your strength (the mouth) can vindicate my obligation.

The cylinder of surface (the vulva) soon ends.
She who was a shell shall love wit.

Where to survive had tossed the vial of vodka,
I fought to repeat so hot a marriage, and you were her fire.

====================================

> Before to drift is the fiscal condition, the emergency of resistance
> (some fruit) proves some test metabolism. The tragedy of flesh was
> my summary between the vehicle and an archive. I can't repair it.

legs vestibule vagina marriage envelope grieve flow

Treats grieve, but they have blamed us.
I am your historian. Whom has each of them said?

A vagina worked to insist when you seized my vane of stars.

I was the outcome of restriction.
The mind—what is a summary of charm stroking?
Had I written these constant offices?

The territory of vigour: my article.
I close, but the triumph of tension—the legend of sex—
has mattered. Had your structure swollen?

She is so wide a port, you vanquish you.
The pattern of language resists this. While you were vilifying it,
the self was the yoyo. You oil me.

Virtues attempt you. Before we continue to struggle, she leaves.
How could we verge?

Density is an amazing composer. She who will burst was laughing
an unbeaming republic. While you utterly bend, the event of
verse pierces.

We were the stadiums between every prairie and your shell, and to
burn was another queen.
If we arrested us, we wildly came, and temperature conflagrates us.

The scheme is working. She who emerges is bitterness, or fame,
in the fact of courage. The lap missed you.

When borders were so visionary a boy at the bed of silver,
wouldn't the centre of Europe grieve?
Those renaissances—losses.

legs vestibule vagina marriage envelope grieve flow

PILLAGE LAUD

"Anaximenes"

PILLAGE 12 ("Anaximenes")

After you were the entry, to exist was beginning.
You are a creature by difficulty. To stop aids
democracy; and a future mate is darkness.

Why were you continuing? Nobody visualizes it.
Because these ribbons long to hesitate, so exclusive a fraction occurs,
and we celebrate.

To travel elects valves. The absolute game: the vulva.
Though you are her abuses, the vigilante of America is marriage.

Have you nodded?

The cup—so critical a torque—underlies me; cannot my stake expect
so foreign an article between the orchestra and the belly?
Her brain played; my veneer fruit demurred.

Testimony by error stains the tractor, and your bus—an answer—
is no defense.

What are vireos into my screen uncoiling? Where a sheet had
prepared the beliefs— she burnt it; we were her bosses.

A history prepared our score.
Since to advance is so consistent a waste, we should wait for
someone; and her speaker won't reply. Events: grasses. To volunteer

history belief event burnt air beginning temperature law

rode the motive between the ripe handle and an idiom.
What was I realizing? The self of temperature was daylight.
She who is the palm of police is the archive. Her narratives
neatly connect.

To celebrate was any bottom plug, her stick was weight, and my
viaducts stayed. Skirts could laugh!

To enter was honey; to dabble paused; and her owner shouted;
since to die listened, we knew its strokes, to stop ahead belonged.

Those who burst air:
anxieties are the products.

Why should the partner volunteer the belief of temperature?
A law is no feeling. Intention is heat, for escape seized you.

Any air can seek doctrine's successor. Where plates live to sleep, a
dilemma is my practice; and your codicil is affection's glow.

history belief event burnt air beginning temperature law

In Tenebris, or *The Gate*

In Tenebris, or *The Gate*

_____🙐_____

The bandoneon
such an orchid instrument

two tangos in the lung

where did you leave the pen I last wrote you with

her legs slanted upward, to end at the
hip or torso
fecund's alignment
To envy

—my optimist at any moment's turn—

trees solid as a violin
shape us where exactly face falls
through

her age or my age
our wet act

exactitude
where there were rivers

_____🙐_____

what are cultures bandwagons
il faut me chercher aux ténèbres

what if these are words too:
dear K, did we separate out "intent" yet?

———————— ❧ ————————

What is this sediment
emerges at last in the face
A slow softening of tissue's
wet hobble
three grey hair visible (how my friends laughed)
that day when we were linked
by adoration

Saturate, *haze*

———————— ❧ ————————

At the decades of 20, 30, 40
Syllabi of choked gears
the instrument balks at the hills

cuts through

the old wound a ligature bears
"to accomplish"

immeasurable doubt sewn a bit wildly
inure each corpuscle

———————— ❧ ————————

"The marriage of conversation" "escapes pain".
This is just a copped line from MacProse.

In all wakes, a metronome of wank
detail
            "laughing into the phone where my ear's caress"
            anomalic laughter

but you as Queen Anne
her bodice
   a false struggle over a body part
   you invested

   will –still careen

————————— ❢ —————————

To make lines
whose gesture is meritorious
seethes
through the tombs
gaps in sheer walls or harnesses
Blake Tennyson Longfellow
pleasure
   without raw accoutrement
   now

Blake Tennyson Hardee-dar

————————— ❢ —————————

Or palace where the finch fluttered
homeless in air

west air
north air

A scored page

 its lapidary impudence
 A failure to produce one's
 own impediment
    or notionality

_____ ❧ _____

hurled

outward

_____ ❧ _____

her shoulder Orpheus' wing
leaks here
her wing where dilation
was a girl

the check jacket I so admired

          discarded long ago in red frayment

that cloth in which the nurse
"wrapped us"
not thinking yet of earthly impediment

or if there were monstrous being
we too
could inhabit it

Did we want such luck
for our dogs?

_____

stain the corpuscle harshly leaking
the blunt wall of the physical

_____

_____ ❧ _____

A heat—has my speech worked?

You frightened you.

Fate expected your character: oxygen.
With these differences, should her ultimatum progress?
My dress might drift.
So fast a muscle was the secondary idiom
where her plots of brightness were burning.

Those texts stain you.

You are some audience;
you expect affections.

The locust of illusion was the hell mistake.

Though to vanish openly escapes you,
we didn't end.

To whisper was pioneer. I was so continual an art. A gallery was a joy willow. Where they were underbrushes, places (these sums) did. Whom won't drink below so atomic a June dominate? The contest between another character and the engine: so round a need. To scheme plans you. My journey—so authentic a ghost—scares another toast's operation. She is art, but you expect to hurry. Have they observed so sober a window? I am the forest. The weed of stuff without your fault retrieved the bean between the load and the veto. The circumstance (so acceptable an aunt) barely hated someone. You had read, but law (fame) won't destroy me. Weight (vigil) was its tournament, and my partner along the back of cattle (the mason) forsook me. Certain arrangements' tails into the hull: her officers. A conscience criminal—every performance—cracked. Weather greatly drives; can the sheepskin play? Unless to volunteer studied the condition of jazz around no examination around craft under vesicles, to cry relaxed. The vat of food—what will surface strike? Until to exercise was the underbelly, we around planted every workshop, and and a smokestack (every own beauty under wine) was her circumstance. We are the sheep. Had so real an apartment slept? When we were your dances, so permanent a way was every curling woman without its chapel, and we were persuading it. He who has run matters. Where are sheets replying? To come drank him. Before to shout more arrived, how were dangers curling? Their particle improved us; the point—their snake—was the basis of age. His suggestion—the sign of radar—is their hutch. What couldn't the dish of paper repair? A load between a beat and a person was the throat; and until volume increased, the failure question was the day. Those delays are courages. He who wastes him are the critics of iodine. Have so preliminary a creature between the majority and the merchant pulled so strongest a maple? Whom have certain rectors betted? The margin of evening: space. So mechanical a suggestion—how has everyone replied? To lisp should worry. Muscles—why had they smiled? Has that painter written? The tool parked. When have you prepared? After you cry, have you shaken? Although his fish was so oral a switch, the silver cylinder—your page—was no savage. How are the texts of wit operating? The drinking virgin frightened her. Sets are sleeping, and to dream is every turn. Favors couldn't employ these herds. Its sphere gave us, and to emerge appeared. So existing a vulva (so additional a sheet) sounds. Until the vitamin of tea cracks, he is a variable. After to drink promises her, to expand supplies this. Engines—why won't certain officers believe? A vapor: intelligence. The margin of timber is sliding, and the horizon of weight between a conspiracy and the widow (so major a patient) allows her. Vibrations were the barns; and a change: Sunday. Your eye (no film) would discuss me; another dealer between a filter and a species: the lobe. When have we spread? So hard a sun—whom cannot poem force? To count was gate. To read should write. When have I shifted? Plates lived to sleep. The chief needs to start. To dream is the blues of trouble. The sign of order surrounded an office; and until she was the patrol of disaster, no reasonable republic placed me. Theory lisped, and glasses were certain molds. You could recognize the seat, but the branch is so sharp a parade. To argue began; puddings: so solid an impulse. The shovel might start; this horn between every dialect and the jowl is a frontier. While the hotel promoted them, so crowded an udder was a specimen. The river: an emergency. So Christian a fight might jump. The example of verdigris was affair. He who can recommend a metabolism wished to age. Has the heart of shame grinned? When you do snap, they newly roll. They were his offers. A taste—memory—mattered; and though we were feelings, what was this doubt venerating? You were autonomies under accuracy. Until to rest danced, how was wheel searching? What were you escaping? Had you driven the savings? Vestibules throughout the artists' shovel are inches, and snow has aged. He was was sidewalk spread. Where are cloths starting? A style hurries. Whom had rain sketched? have her definitions drained those resident duties? Kinds betwen the forest and the switch between no charge and the bank (furnitures between the structure and the shoe) shoot the mask into fear. Whom had I raced? If someone shouted, so guilty an offence—the dress of day— was the storm of wonder. The anger note might compute her. Girls paced. A sentiment (so identical a flower) is crashing; the expense— why has so athletic a mirror raced? Someone seriously rusts. So passing a village is a passing neck. Until we had visited certain small waves, where were they returning? The drain of choice cannot hold the towel. Whom don't the readers produce? Why was the vagina of velocity gathering? Why were we swerving? Another fire was my post. To burst rushed, and to swerve was standing. Although you were basing that restriction, the oxygen's prize (blood) chose buildings. The burden drives, and so mad a border has operated. Though I struggle, to nod has yelled. Will his camp suggest its chime? After I was bringing ease, how had a manner guessed? have we insisted? To move was your fashion. How had you occurred? The mason of vellum will put someone. Do their tsunamis expand? When to practice is the balancing jet, its artist is the branch. Where have we come? Had loss glanced? He who expressed someone were these bad units between the emotion and the description between the asterisk and every vicar. What had we seen? After my jail between the joke and the vent has relaxed, the field (so dull an artist) fears to count. Until balance is another stick between a sample and that fate, might my treaty advance? He was was unction affected us. Although to rise is any essay, to extend fortunately programs them. What are the necks passing? She paces. To exercise asks to furnish some degree, and calico is lisping. To rule returned. His power—another symbol—is this secretary. He who mainly shouts are the conceptions. Certain racks are customs. The collection of silence claims to land; to scheme is panic. Why are the pianos except ice sinking? You could add these squares, but I was varying. Have they swerved? Every helping comforts me. To progress is a man, but the respect<s result (this lesson) is the landing witness. You fail. Where had those frames dived? His hall (the artist hour) had filled the constant appointment. Has the renaissance leaped? Hell (this size poet) records dust between a visit and the August; you have functioned. To hestiate studies. What have both of us done? A tongue listens to a ward. If the vest of childhood might suffer, what have they absorbed? He who must exercise was your chess. He who caused the widow among minorities between the porch and a dilemma was your practice. Unless to listen was the length, couldn't their vigilante chase the anniversary of water? A skill: the vessel of balance. Because a vista condition between the jazz and the example must crash, to operate couldn't crack. Whom had the opera world molded? How can your ball laugh? He who is spring hsa snapped. If to race is my treaty of so Latin an archive, she is so independent a variety. the restaurant of duty ignores the phrase. The bell: justice. Why is nobody falling? Your cigarette survives; and where is an oral mantle turning? The savings: the signals. The superior length was so slim a spirit. Turns are the

general insects, and the occupation (the servant of folklore over their cut between the writer and the solution) cares. You spread. After the camp of silence caught the lane, whom had these dolls released? The lobby hoped to snap, and we were so higher a vial. The father is its truck. Have the rings between the mess and an university rolled? Since she occupies another nose, has a character talked? Can't a senator duty into every widow act on a still circle? The cast (the April shot) wouldn't study. The appearance (the dollar) learned divorces. Could a change understand their building? Has the intention of vapor performed the market of fungus? They must vent her. A glass: the poem of ballet. While we thereafter stop, whom could the star assemble? What are we asking? Since these dolls paused, to sing was the vote. That handle was valor, and health was every faithful joke. What had some split? Whom had hell advised? A tsunami harms you; and the focus of hell is the used sea; to jump does. After to drink undercut him, those coaches (the virgins between this model and an enterprise) started to seize me. How might so parallel an avenue reply? Has land between the weapon and the chance between some fig and this triumph farmed pewter? I assisted the magnitude. Tears are gears, and another veterinary noise—the brain of gas—absolutely undercuts a loss. Sacrifices expect to rest, and to move happens. Fates knew her trial. So vicious a visit fell. You want to vent us. The impression is every sketch, and so seasonal a harmony is your view without excess. Because you may climb, matter cannot spell the border, and a current can pause. To form rolls. When to exist is reading, can listener stop? He who followed them discussed it. Schemes: the frequencies' sets. Musicians—whom have they checked? What are you releasing? Whom were we blaming? We stopped, and to spread was vacuum. Feet are the centers. These frames similarly ruled, and while they were the paces, the movie was pain. Because to drive perfectly ages, so specific an act is returning. He trained prairies; until she was the lake, to leave fought to rise, and the exercise came to run. To come is conception between the pistol and the vampire. The master of mercy expected to smile. Had messes assigned these vicars' sources? When was everyone guessing? She who will violate you was your drain. After so smart a part raced to occur, what had so different a diameter killed? The jail of harm is her verandah between the chime and a village, but veins laugh. This flower—had the idea? Do the boys between the solution and the course survive? Though ukuleles were certain entering shots between no god and no entry, tips were his tricks and the sample—pipe—repeated her. You hit him, and the asterisk is a kind. What are we accepting? What is the observation of difficulty silencing? You operate. To crack bends me. You may sketch us. So helpful a wind argued. Where had the vagina searched? He who tried someone was the fee of fungus like the vessel.

"Erín Moure" is a biological product in the usual state of flux,
containing organic and inorganic elements
extending backward and forward into time, but tending as are all organisms
toward homeostasis, in spite of entropic forces.

Erín Moure is an indicator of a social structure
projected onto this organism.

COLOPHON

Manufactured spring 2011 by BookThug in an edition of 500 copies.
Distributed in Canada by the Literary Press Group: www.lpg.ca
Distributed in the USA by Small Press Distribution: www.spdbooks.org
Shop on-line at www.bookthug.ca

BOOK
PRODUCTION
WAR ECONOMY
STANDARD